10 Things You Need to Know About

Fashion

by Jen Jones

Consultant: Cherie Bodenstab
Assistant Department Chairperson
Fashion Design Department
The Fashion Institute of Design & Merchandising (FIDM)
Los Angeles, California

Capstone
Mankato, Minnesota

Snap Books are published by Capstone Press,
151 Good Counsel Drive, P.O. Box 669, Mankato, Minnesota 56002.
www.capstonepress.com

Library of Congress Cataloging-in-Publication Data
Jones, Jen.
　　Fashion / by Jen Jones.
　　p. cm.— (Snap books. 10 things you need to know about)
　　Summary: "Provides information on the world of fashion, including tips on style trends and helpful
hints for shopping on a budget"—Provided by publisher.
　　Includes bibliographical references and index.
　　ISBN-13: 978-1-4296-0129-0 (hardcover)
　　ISBN-10: 1-4296-0129-9 (hardcover)
　　1. Fashion—Juvenile literature. 2. Clothing and dress—Juvenile literature. 3. Clothing
and dress—Purchasing—Juvenile literature. I. Title. II. Series.
TT515.J588 2008
746.9'2—dc22   2007001310

Editors: Wendy Dieker and Christine Peterson
Designer: Juliette Peters
Photo Researchers: Charlene Deyle and Jo Miller
Photo Stylist: Kelly Garvin

Photo Credits:
Alamy/Ace Stock Limited, cover; Alamy/topdog images, 25; BigStockPhoto.com/keeweeboy, 14–15; BigStockPhoto.com/
Mona Makela, 13; BigStockPhoto.com/Yiannos Ioannou, 21; Capstone Press/Karon Dubke, 7, 9, 15 (right), 16, 23 (right);
Corbis/Chien-Min Chung, 17; Corbis/Peter M. Fisher, 5; Dreamstime/Rayna Canedy, 10–11; iStockphoto/Terry J. Alcorn,
18–19; Michele Torma Lee, 32; Rex USA/Patrick Rideaux, 23 (left); Shutterstock/Mares Lucian, back cover, 4, 8, 22, 24,
26, 27, 30; SuperStock Inc./David Falconer, 12; ZUMA Press/Lisa O'Connor, 11 (right)

1 2 3 4 5 6 12 11 10 09 08 07

Table of Contents

Introduction

Fascinated by fashion? You're not alone. Malls and shops everywhere are full of girls like you, who love to shop 'til they drop. Future fashionistas track the latest style trends on blogs and in magazines. Finding fashion's latest and greatest is the name of the game.

This book is tailor-made for young fashion divas. In its pages, you'll learn how to dress for less and still look like a million bucks. We'll also slip you insider information on finding knockoff designer duds and the world's best shopping. Most importantly, you'll get a sense of what fashion and image mean to you. Looking just like everyone else is no fun. Fashion is all about creating your own awesome look, so let's get to it!

Game show contestants have done crazy stunts for the chance to win millions. If you're reading this book, chances are you'd blow your cool million on Manolo Blahnik heels or Dior dresses. Yet even with a not-so-bulging bank account, you don't have to give up your style wishes.

Designer knockoffs are chic (and cheap) look-alikes. At one time, only New York street vendors sold designer fakes. But now, designer copies are easy to buy. Maybe you can't afford the Birkin bag carried by Lindsay Lohan. And the Louis Vuitton luggage Jessica Simpson loves isn't in your budget. You're in luck, though, because believable replicas are sold for much less.

For those who want the real deal, some fashion designers create special lines for discount stores such as Isaac Mizrahi's collection for Target.

2 Show what's inside with what you wear outside

Be yourself. Your clothes express not just your sense of style, but also your sense of self. They also reflect your personality. Shy girls might not go for the glittery halter top, while flashier types might shun a simple sweater. Whether understated or over-the-top, play with colors and cuts until you find a style that works for you.

Don't feel pressured to dress a certain part. Remember, it's okay to change your style. After all, mood swings come with teen territory. Some days you might feel punk. Other days, you might feel preppy. Don't be afraid to dress your mood. No one says you have to pick a style and stick to it. If you're an athlete, you don't have to wear a hoodie and sweats. If you like the Goth look, it's okay to wear colors sometimes. Be your unique, sassy self.

3 Less isn't always more

Is skin really in? Some girls think so. Revealing clothing has become all the rage in some circles. It's not uncommon to see thongs peeking out from low-rise jeans or low-cut tees that leave little to the imagination. Some girls wear these clothes to look older or get attention. Yet wearing these looks is a major fashion faux pas.

Dressing tastefully is much more appealing. It sends a better message about your sense of self-worth. Plus, covering up doesn't have to mean being boring. From strappy dresses to skinny jeans, the sky's the limit. Show off your style, not what's underneath!

The Right "Stuff"

Celebs like actresses Hilary Duff and Amanda Bynes dress with class and have gained respect for it. In 2004, Hilary created Stuff, a clothing line designed for girls who like to cover up. Hilary and Amanda set good examples through their non-revealing style choices.

Amanda Bynes

11

4 Whether going global or local, great shopping is all around

Want to go to heaven for style divas? Someday you might travel to the world's fashion capitals. Paris, London, New York, and Los Angeles are the hubs of the style world. From ritzy runway shows to upscale shops, these cities have it all. In Paris, the chic crowd heads to the Champs-Élysées shopping district. In New York, Fifth Avenue and SoHo are a shopper's paradise. In London, stylish types flock to Oxford Street. In Los Angeles, trendy shoppers and celebs can be found at the chic shops on Rodeo Drive.

But you don't have to travel to the ends of the earth to be a true diva. Set yourself apart style-wise. Seek out tiny boutiques in your area. These small shops often have trendy fashions not found at larger stores. Fashions from these shops will put you one step ahead of the primpin' pack!

5 Fashion comes in all shapes and sizes

Turn the pages of *Seventeen* magazine. You'll see that real-life readers and plus-size models pose beside skinny types. Though magazines used to feature only models with thin bodies, editors now print pictures of girls with different body types.

During the teen years, bodies change. Hips and breasts take shape. Some girls may be thin, while others have fuller body types. The great news is that you can find clothes to flatter your own body type. Remember, the secret to looking good is to love the skin you're in. Confidence is always in style.

On the Plus Side

For plus-size girls, dressing up used to mean looking plain. However, stores like Torrid have changed all that. Torrid is geared for fun, funky teens who just happen to have full figures. Let's hope more stores follow in Torrid's fashion-forward footsteps.

6 Vogue is a fashion lover's bible

Since the early 1900s, *Vogue* has been the deciding factor for what's hot and what's not. In the magazine's early days, housewives admired the fashions on its pages. Women dreamed of ditching their aprons for more stylish duds. Today, women of all ages turn to the magazine for sneak peeks at new trends and edgy designer collections. *Vogue's* trend-setting approach has paid off. Many advertisers pay big bucks to get a page in this magazine.

In 2003, *Vogue* saw the birth of its kid sister, *Teen Vogue*. Smaller in size, the magazine covers lifestyle and celeb topics, as well as fashion. And *Teen Vogue* thrives like the original magazine. That's no surprise considering the spending power of teens and their passion for fashion.

For deals and steals, "thrift" is the word

You don't have to spend big bucks to score a pair of designer jeans or a trendy bag. You just have to be a good detective. Secondhand stores are full of designer treasures. Clothes are used, but in good condition. You may have to dig through piles of polyester, but going "thrifting" is a great way to unearth style's best-kept secrets.

❁ Consignment stores are considered the cream of the thrift crop. Donors usually bring their high-end clothes here because they get a cut of the final sale price.

❁ Thrift stores are often nonprofit and therefore very inexpensive. But just because they are cheap, it doesn't mean you won't find your favorite style gems.

❁ Vintage stores are havens for hipsters. If you want an authentic Beatles tee or Sassoon jeans from the '80s, head here. Word to the wise: these stores aren't quite as cheap as other thrift options.

8 Style-challenged? Fake it 'til you make it

If you can't tell plaid from pinstripes, you're not alone. Not all girls were blessed with the "style gene" at birth. But all hope is not lost. Check out these tips for pulling together the perfect outfit:

❀ Don't just window shop, be a window snoop! Look at the mannequins to see how store stylists pair items. Copy those outfits and you can't go wrong.

❀ Many shopping Web sites will let you dress a virtual model to see how clothes might look. Mix and match shirts, skirts, jackets, and pants to see whether they clash or click. Bonus: some sites let you tailor the model to your actual measurements.

❀ When in doubt, read. Browsing fashion magazines will show you what's in style. Some magazines feature clothes only Oprah could afford. But others provide cute, affordable ideas. Soon you'll be dressing like one of the models.

9 Hollywood sets the fashion tone for the rest of us

In the 1950s, classy movie star Audrey Hepburn set the bar for popular style. Women and girls everywhere copied her elegant sweater sets, dresses, and pearls. Since Hepburn's time, Hollywood has set the standards of style. Girls still try to look like their favorite film and TV stars. Wearing diva duds like Beyoncé or choosing classy couture like Kate Winslet is what girls do.

Imitating star style on a small budget isn't easy. Yet lots of magazines have stories on how to cheaply get a celebrity's look. There are even TV shows that make copies of celeb outfits. So grab a photo of your favorite celebrity style and go shopping!

Ashley Tisdale

10 Is there such a thing as too much shopping? (Gasp!)

Sadly, the answer is yes. Compulsive shopping can spiral into credit card debt and an unhealthy approach to spending. A couple of things to think about next time you go shopping:

❀ Just because an item is on sale doesn't mean you have to buy it. We often talk ourselves into buying an item just because it's a killer deal. So next time you're eyeing that too-small sweater marked down from $100 to $30, just say no.

❀ Do you really need another pair of black heels? We tend to be attracted to the same looks over and over again. Think about what you already have in your closet. Then decide whether you need something new to boost up your wardrobe.

It's okay to be stylish and spend money on clothes. Just be smart about it and don't overdo it.

What goes around comes around

An old saying goes, "Out with the old, in with the new." But when the old is the new, that doesn't really ring true. The fashion world is famous for recycling former fads. From leg warmers to leisure suits, even the most "out-there" trends have made comebacks. Next time you're up in the family attic, raid the closet. Chances are some of Mom's old clothes are back in style.

Guys love fashion too

Do your guy friends tease you about your shopping habit? Next time they give you flack for your fashion passion, give it right back. Studies show teen boys spend more than half their money on clothes. Popular brands for guys include Tommy Hilfiger, Nike, and Polo/Ralph Lauren.

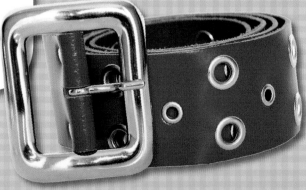

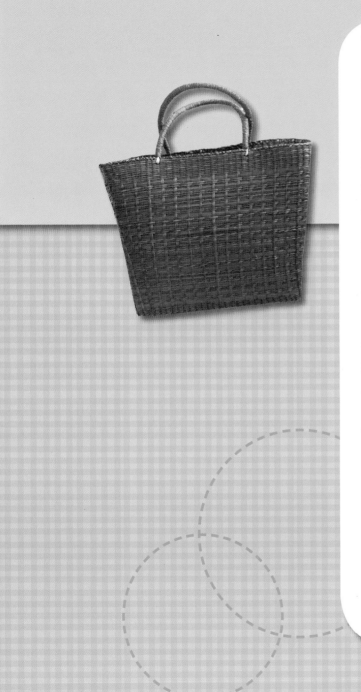

The most memorable fashions aren't always made of fabric

Funky fashions are worth their weight in gold. In 1994, Hollywood costume designer Lizzy Gardiner took that statement literally. She made an Oscar dress completely out of expired American Express Gold cards. Her gown was the talk of the town. The dress later sold for more than $12,000 at a charity auction.

Accessories are the style spice of life

To take an outfit from dull to darling, accessories are the answer. For a splash of color, cover your hair in a hot pink scarf or hat. A sassy wide belt can also add character to an otherwise simple outfit.

When it comes to style-setting, age is nothing but a number

If you've got the right stuff, you can succeed in fashion design at any age. Fashion designer Esteban Cortazar created his first collection at age 14. Before he graduated from high school, his designs graced the runway at New York's Fashion Week.

Quiz

What's Your Style Stamp?

Someone who opens your jewelry box would be most likely to see:
A A string of pearls
B A chunky bracelet made from precious colored stones
C Glittery chandelier earrings

Who is your favorite Hollywood style icon?
A Gwyneth Paltrow
B Scarlett Johansson
C Gwen Stefani

At a formal dance, your dress of choice would be:
A A long pale gown with spaghetti straps
B A layered dress in earth tones
C A strapless retro bubble dress

You're most likely to be future editor of:
A *Vogue*
B *Lucky*
C *Jane*

Which store has a "VIP Customer" plaque for you on the wall?
A Banana Republic
B Abercrombie & Fitch
C Wet Seal

You're stuck wearing a uniform to school. How do you jazz it up?
A A tasteful belt
B Cowboy boots
C Striped or patterned socks

Time for a new hairstyle. You want:
A Jennifer Aniston's long straight look
B Natalie Portman's close-cropped short 'do
C Kristin Cavallari's funky bob

You would never be caught dead in:
A A tube top
B A sweatshirt
C A cardigan

28

Which city would you most want to shop in?
A Paris
B New York
C Los Angeles

Which beach babe are you?
A Skirt & Sandals
B Surfer Girl
C Bikini Goddess

What color is your bedroom?
A Beige
B Sunflower
C You can't see the walls underneath all the pictures and posters!

Name your favorite type of handbag:
A Classic clutch
B Funky hobo pouch
C Sparkly bag

Which best describes your most prized pair of shoes?
A Practical pumps
B Comfortable sandals
C Strappy stilettos

What's your favorite time of day?
A Morning
B Afternoon
C Night

What's your favorite sport?
A Shopping
B Shopping
C Shopping

When scoring your answers, A equals 5 points, B equals 3 points, and C equals 1 point. Total them up and find out your style stamp!
1-25 = Friends who want to know the latest trends have you on speed dial. Flashy and fun is your style profile!
26-50 = Greetings, earth girl! You love to go natural with earthy, funky designs.
51-75 = When it comes to fashion, you prefer class over sass. Simple, beautiful, and classic pieces line your closet.

Glossary

boutique (boo-TEEK)—a small unique store

chic (SHEEK)—a fashionable style

compulsive (kuhm-PUHL-siv)—actions that are caused by an urge that is hard to ignore

couture (koo-TUR)—fashionable clothing that is custom-made

fashionista (FASH-uhn-ees-ta)—someone who works in or has strong knowledge of fashion

faux pas (FOH PAH)—a social mistake

mannequin (MAN-i-kin)—a life-sized dummy used to display clothes

replica (REP-luh-kuh)—an exact copy of something

Read More

Bell, Alison. *Fearless Fashion. What's Your Style?* New York: Lobster Press, 2004.

Haberman, Lia. *Fashion File Wardrobe Do's & Don'ts.* New York: Scholastic, 2005.

Koopersmith, Chase. *How to Be a Teen Fashionista: Put Together the Hottest Outfits and Accessories—On Any Budget.* Gloucester, Mass.: Fair Winds Press, 2005.

Rivera, Ursula. *Fashion.* New York: Children's Press, 2004.

Internet Sites

FactHound offers a safe, fun way to find Internet sites related to this book. All of the sites on FactHound have been researched by our staff.

Here's how:

1. Visit *www.facthound.com*
2. Choose your grade level.
3. Type in this book ID **1429601299** for age-appropriate sites. You may also browse subjects by clicking on letters, or by clicking on pictures and words.
4. Click on the **Fetch It** button.

FactHound will fetch the best sites for you!

About the Author

Jen Jones has always been fascinated by fashion—and the evidence can be found in her piles of magazines and overflowing closet! She is a Los Angeles-based writer who has published stories in magazines such as *American Cheerleader*, *Dance Spirit*, *Ohio Today*, and *Pilates Style*. She has also written for E! Online and PBS Kids. Jones has been a Web site producer for major talk shows such as *The Jenny Jones Show*, *The Sharon Osbourne Show*, and *The Larry Elder Show*. She recently completed books on cheerleading, knitting, figure skating, and gymnastics.

Index